Do You Know Your Wine?
Part 2

The Ultimate World Wine Quiz

Author Val Policella

ISBN: 1976296153

ISBN-13: 978-1976296154

Do You Know Your Wine?

CONTENTS

Introduction

This book is a collection of wine quizzes for amateur wine enthusiasts designed to test your knowledge of wines and wine related trivia by country of origin.

I have had several great evenings with family and friends over the years whilst sharing a fabulous bottle of wine or two!

Why not open a bottle or two with friends and family or host your own wine evening, pick up this book, put your quizmaster's hat on and away you go.

Included within this book is a section for recording your own personal wine tasting notes and recording your personal favourite wines.

I hope you enjoy these quizzes as much as I have.

Do You Know Your Wine?

USA

1. Where does the USA rank amongst the largest wine producing countries of the world?

2. California accounts for how much of the wine production in the USA?

   A. 28%

   B. 69%

   C. 89%

3. How many commercial vineyards does the USA have?

4. True or false? Wine production in the state of California is greater than the amount of wine produced in Australia.

5. Which red wine grape variety is the most planted in the Napa Valley?

6. Which white wine grape variety is the most planted in the State of Texas?

7. Where does the State of Washington rank in the USA for wine production?

8. Which is New York's largest wine growing region?

9. How many grape varieties are grown in the State of Washington?

10. The Sonoma County wine region is in which State?

VAL POLICELLA

CHILE

1. True or false? The Spanish introduced vines in to Chile in the 16th century

2. How many wine growing regions are there in Chile?

3. Which Spanish style sweet wine is now produced in the Huasco Valley?

4. Which type of wine is the Casablanca Valley wine region primarily known for producing?

    A. Sparkling

    B. Red

    C. White

5. What is the name of the Brandy made by distilling fermented grape juice in the Atacama wine making region?

6. How does Chile rank amongst the largest wine exporting countries in the world?

   A. 5th

   B. 6th

   C. 7th

7. Which are the 3 most common grape varieties grown in Chile?

   A. Sauvignon blanc, Merlot, Zinfandel

   B. Merlot, Malbec, Cabernet Sauvignon

   C. Cabernet Sauvignon, Merlot, Carmenère

8. A "Gran Vino" must be aged for a minimum of how many years?

9. What is the minimum alcohol percentage an exported Chilean white wine must be?

   A. 10.5% ABV

   B. 11% ABV

   C. 12% ABV

10. Chilean wine is predominantly red

wine. What percentage of vineyards is dedicated to growing white grapes for producing white wines?

A. 13%

B. 26%

C. 31%

ARGENTINA

1. The Mendoza wine region accounts for how much of the total wine production in Argentina?

   A. 39%

   B. 67%

   C. 70%

2. Which grape variety of French origin is grown more in Argentina than any other place in the world?

   A. Malbec

   B. Cereza

   C. Barbera

3. How does Argentina rank for wine production in South America?

   A. 1st

   B. 2nd

C. 3rd

4. How many wine regions are there in Argentina?

5. Where does Argentina rank in the world for wine production?

    A. 3rd

    B. 5th

    C. 6th

6. Which red grape variety is the 2nd most widely grown in Argentina?

    A. Syrah

    B. Bonarda

    C. Rabosa

7. Which out of the three Torrontés white wine grape varieties are the most widely planted?

    A. Torrontés Riojano

    B. Torrontés Sanjuanino

C. Torrontés Mendocino

8. Which wine region has the longest history of wine production in Argentina?

9. Are Argentinian wines considered to be New World or Old World wines?

10. Which wine region is the most southerly in Argentina?

VAL POLICELLA

AUSTRALIA

1. How much of the wine produced in Australia is consumed domestically?

    A. 25%

    B. 35%

    C. 40%

2. How does Australia rank amongst the largest wine exporting countries in the world?

3. How many different grape varieties are used commercially for wine making in Australia?

    A. 58

    B. 96

    C. 130

4. Which white grape variety is the most planted in Australia?

5. How much was the most expensive bottle of Australian wine sold for in 2012?

A. $50000

B. $73000

C. $168000

6. True or false? The United Kingdom imports more wine from Australia than it does from France.

7. The Coonawarra wine region is known for which type of wine?

    A. Cabernet Sauvignon

    B. Riesling

    C. Shiraz

8. The Australian state of Tasmania has how many wine growing regions?

    A. 5

    B. 6

    C. 7

9. True or false? The most common grown grape variety in Tasmania is Pinot Gris.

10. The region of Mudgee predominantly produces which type of wine?

A. Sparkling wine

B. Red wine

C. White wine

NEW ZEALAND

1. The Auckland wine region predominantly produces which type of wine?

    A. Red wine

    B. White wine

    C. Sparkling wine

2. The vines in the Auckland wine region are grown in which type of soil?

    A. Terra Rosa

    B. Limestone

    C. Heavy clay

3. True or false? New Zealand produces more wine per annum than Portugal?

4. Which is the largest wine producing region in New Zealand?

    A. Marlborough

B. Nelson

C. Wellington

5. Which is the oldest wine producing region in New Zealand?

A. Gisborne

B. Hawkes Bay

C. Northland

6. True or false? The Central Otago wine region is the world's most southern commercial wine growing region.

7. Central Otago is best known for which wine?

A. Pinot Noir

B. Shiraz

C. Cabernet Sauvignon

8. Which wine region produces the highest quantity of sparkling wine?

A. Auckland

B. Northland

C. Marlborough

9. Which grape is New Zealand's most widely planted variety?

   A. Merlot

   B. Sauvignon Blanc

   C. Chardonnay

10. What is New Zealand's 4th most widely planted white grape variety?

   A. Riesling

   B. Pinot Blanc

   C. Chenin Blanc

VAL POLICELLA

SOUTH AFRICA

1. How does South Africa rank amongst the wine producers in the world?

   A. 5th

   B. 9th

   C. 13th

2. True or false? Stellenbosch is the oldest wine region in South Africa.

3. How much of the Countries total wine production is the Stellenbosch region responsible for?

   A. 14%

   B. 29%

   C. 67%

4. The Stellenbosch region is renowned for which type of wine?

   A. Red wine

B. White wine

C. Sparkling wine

5. What is the name given to the South African fortified wine?

6. What is the minimum alcohol level these wines must be?

A. 16-19%

B. 16-20%

C. 16.5-22%

7. The most widely grown red grape variety in South Africa is?

A. Grenache

B. Cabernet Sauvignon

C. Cabernet Franc

8. True or false? The Cape Winelands is the largest wine growing region in South Africa?

9. True or false? Route 61 leads through several wine regions and is known as

the longest wine route in the world.

10. True or false? The Worcester district which is part of the Breede River Valley accounts for ½ of the total wine production of the whole of South Africa.

MOLDOVA

1. How does "vin de casa" translate?

2. How many wine growing regions are there in Moldova?

   A. 3

   B. 4

   C. 5

3. The Purcari wine region is most famous for which type of wine?

   A. Sparkling wine

   B. White wine

   C. Red wine

4. True or false? The Mileștii Mici winery has the largest wine collection in the world.

5. Moldova's state owned Cricova wine cellars hold the private collection of

which famous Russian person?

6. True or false? This famous Russian person (answer number 5) also spent their 6oth birthday at the Cricova winery.

7. The Cricova winery is also notably known for producing which type of wine?

   A. Red wine

   B. White wine

   C. Sparkling wine

8. Is the majority of wine produced in Moldova for export or domestic consumption?

9. How does Moldova rank amongst the wine producers in the world?

   A. 13th

   B. 20th

   C. 23rd

10. What percentage of vineyards in Moldova are white grape varieties?

A. 70%

B. 80%

C. 85%

SERBIA

1. When is the grape harvesting season in Serbia?

   A. July-September

   B. June-August

   C. July-October

2. How does Serbia rank amongst the wine producers in the world?

   A. 19th

   B. 23rd

   C. 29th

3. How many wine growing regions are there in Serbia?

   A. 5

   B. 22

   C. 42

4. How much of overall production is red wine?

    A. 36%

    B. 48%

    C. 75%

5. True or false? Smederevka wine is normally drunk mixed with soda.

6. Is the Prokupac grape a red or white grape variety?

7. Which type of wine is produced from the Tamjanika grape

    A. Red wine

    B. White wine

    C. Sparkling wine

8. The Negotin wine region is notable for which wine?

    A. Muscat

    B. Riesling

   C. Chardonnay

9. How many grapes do the Serbian vineyards produce annually?

   A. 350,000 tons

   B. 400,000 tons

   C. 425,000 tons

10. What is the annual international wine fair held in Belgrade called?

VAL POLICELLA

CANADA

1. How does Canada rank amongst the wine producers in the world?

   A. 5th

   B. 14th

   C. 28th

2. The Canadian wine industry vinifies imported grape juice and concentrate. How are these wines labeled?

3. The Okanagan Valley wine region is the 2nd largest wine region in Canada. Which type of wine is this region most notably known for?

   A. Ice wine

   B. Fortified wine

   C. Sparkling wine

4. How many bottles of wine does the Canadian wine industry produce each

year?

    A. 185 million

    B. 200 million

    C. 220 million

5. Canadian wine industry sales represent how much of the wine sold across Canada?

    A. 25%

    B. 30%

    C. 35%

6. The 1st commercially produced Canadian Ice wine was released in which year?

    A. 1978

    B. 1980

    C. 1989

7. True or false? Canada is the largest Ice wine producer in the world.

8. Which white grape variety is most planted in the British Columbia wine region?

    A. Pinot Blanc

    B. Pinot Gris

    C. Sauvignon Blanc

9. Which red grape variety is most planted in the British Columbia wine region?

    A. Merlot

    B. Pinot Noir

    C. Cabernet Franc

10. In the Ontario wine region, what is the maximum amount of imported grape juice or concentrate allowed to be used in "Cellared in Canada" wine blends?

    A. 60%

    B. 65%

    C. 70%

HUNGARY

1. How many wine growing regions are there in Hungary?

    A. 12

    B. 22

    C. 32

2. Which type of wine accounts for 75% of Hungarian wine production?

    A. Sparkling wine

    B. Red wine

    C. White wine

3. The Tokaji wine region in the North East is famous for which type of wine?

    A. Sparkling wine

    B. Dessert wine

    C. Fortified wine

4. The king of Hungary (Franz Joseph 1848-1916) sent which queen 972 bottles of Tokaji Aszú wine for her 81st birthday?(1 bottle for every month she had lived)

5. True or false? The Ezerjó grape used to make Hungarian dessert wine originates from Romania.

6. Which type of wine is the Villány wine region known for?

   A. Red wine

   B. White wine

   C. Rosé wine

7. White grape varieties account for how much of the total vineyard plantings in Hungary?

   A. 57%

   B. 63%

   C. 67%

8. The Sopron wine region mainly

produces which type of wine?

A. Red wine

B. Fortified wine

C. Ice wine

9. True or false? The Pannonhalma-Sokoró wine region produces an Ice wine from Riesling grapes.

10. True or false? The Irsai Oliver grape variety originates from Hungary

PERSONAL WINE TASTING NOTES

Do You Know Your Wine?

Do You Know Your Wine?

PERSONAL FAVOURITE WINES

VAL POLICELLA

Do You Know Your Wine?

Do You Know Your Wine?

QUIZ ANSWERS

USA

1. 4th

2. 89%

3. 3000

4. True

5. Cabernet Sauvignon

6. Chardonnay

7. 2nd

8. Finger Lakes

9. 80

10. California

CHILE

1. True

2. 5

3. Paxarette

4. White wine

5. Pisco

6. 5th

7. Cabernet Sauvignon, Merlot, Carmenère

8. 6 years

9. 12% ABV

10. 26%

ARGENTINA

1. 70%

2. Malbec

3. 1st

4. 5

5. 6th

6. Bonarda / Douce Noir

7. Torrontés Riojano

8. La Rioja

9. New World

10. Rio Negro

AUSTRALIA

1. 40%

2. 4th

3. 130

4. Chardonnay

5. $168000

6. True

7. Cabernet Sauvignon

8. 7

9. False, it's Pinot Noir

10. Red wine

NEW ZEALAND

1. Red wine

2. Heavy clay

3. False

4. Marlborough

5. Hawkes Bay

6. True

7. Pinot Noir

8. Marlborough

9. Sauvignon Blanc

10. Riesling

SOUTH AFRICA

1. 9th

2. False, Constantia is the oldest

3. 14%

4. Red wine

5. Cape port

6. 16.5-22%

7. Cabernet Sauvignon

8. True

9. False, it's Route 62

10. False

MOLDOVA

1. Homemade wine

2. 4

3. Red wine

4. True

5. Vladmir Putin

6. False, he spent his 50th birthday at the winery

7. The Kodrinskoie-sparkling

8. Export

9. 20th

10. 70%

SERBIA

1. July-October

2. 19th

3. 22

4. 36%

5. True

6. Red

7. White wine

8. Muscat

9. 425,000 tons

10. Beo Wine Fair

CANADA

1. 28th

2. Cellared in Canada

3. Ice wine

4. 220 million

5. 30%

6. 1978

7. True

8. Pinot Gris

9. Merlot

10. 60%

HUNGARY

1. 22

2. White wine

3. Dessert wine

4. Queen Victoria

5. False, it's Hungarian

6. Red wine

7. 67%

8. Red wine

9. True

10. True

Do You Know Your Wine?

www.ingramcontent.com/pod-product-compliance
Lightning Source LLC
Chambersburg PA
CBHW070828240726
48654CB00007B/508